THE WISDOM OF
CALL THE MIDWIFE

THE WISDOM OF CALL THE MIDWIFE

Words of inspiration
from the Sisters and midwives
of Nonnatus House

FOREWORD BY HEIDI THOMAS

WEIDENFELD & NICOLSON

First published in Great Britain in 2020 by Weidenfeld & Nicolson
an imprint of The Orion Publishing Group Ltd
Carmelite House, 50 Victoria Embankment
London EC4Y 0DZ

An Hachette UK Company

1 3 5 7 9 10 8 6 4 2

Foreword and Text compilation: Heidi Thomas
Set Photographers: Kevin Baker, Joss Barratt, Laurence Cendrowicz,
Gareth Gatrell, Mark Johnson, Nicky Johnston, Sophie Mutevelian,
Laura Radford, Aimee Spinks, Ollie Upton, Kelly Walsh.

Call the Midwife
A Neal Street Production for the BBC

A CIP catalogue record for this book is
available from the British Library.

ISBN (Hardback) 978 1 4746 1942 4
ISBN (eBook) 978 1 4746 1943 1

Printed in Italy

www.weidenfeldandnicolson.co.uk
www.orionbooks.co.uk

CONTENTS

Foreword 1

FOREWORD
by Heidi Thomas

Drama is about relationships. Love stories, crime stories, comedy and tragedy are all fired by the ties between others and ourselves. With nursing at its heart, *Call the Midwife* depends on human interaction more than most shows. However, it is not just what is seen on screen that matters. Ever since the series launched in 2012, our connection with our audience has been our lifeblood.

Based on a trilogy of memoirs by retired nurse Jennifer Worth, *Call the Midwife* initially looked set to be a beautiful but small-scale series, and was launched with little fanfare. To the delight of all involved, it made a massive and surprising impact, with eight million viewers tuning in, and wanting more. The letters, emails, messages and tweets we received were so passionate and so generous that we not only carried on, but resolved to make the very best drama that we could.

Sadly Jennifer, whom I admired and loved, died shortly before we started filming Series 1. There was enough of her trilogy left to give us quite a lot of Series 2, but the remaining stories would not last forever. Without new contributions from her gifted pen, we had to look further afield for fresh material. Medical and newspaper archives were an obvious and exciting resource, as were midwifery textbooks of the period. Our fans also made an unexpected contribution. Moved by what they had seen already, they wrote to us in their droves, outlining their own experiences as midwives, mothers and nurses in the 1950s. When we used these personal insights to flesh out our own exacting historical research, the world of Poplar felt more exciting and replete with potential than ever.

As the creator of the series, and its main writer, nothing gives me greater pleasure than the fact that our relationship with the audience has always been a two-way street. Over time, it has become clear that *Call the Midwife* is a show over which our audience feels a sense of ownership. Retired midwives and nurses donate their badges, their buckles and their scarves. Some fans ask us to send them our vintage knitting patterns, others simply knit and send us baby clothes. Viewers write to ask where Shelagh buys her glasses, to say they wore Valerie's floral coat to their sister's wedding in 1965, or to tell us that their mum wore bright-blue eyeshadow like Violet.

Others share their deepest pain. They recount their experience of infant loss and stillbirth, of surviving cancer, of sitting with loved ones as they pass away. We hear from women who gave up babies for adoption, and from adopted babies, long grown and known by other names. I am always deeply moved by the way in which they watch the show to see their past reflected back, and their present given meaning. In short, our stories are their stories too.

Over the years, *Call the Midwife* has evolved and grown. Lovely Jenny Lee cycled away under the viaduct, and innocent, impulsive Barbara came to take her place. The Turners married. Trixie's glossy outer shell cracked open, exposing her fragile core, and formidable Nurse Crane revealed her own past sadness, and her hidden depths. When Reggie, who has Down's syndrome, was taken in by the Buckles, and Lucille arrived from Jamaica, our world expanded further. The Pill made its debut. Meanwhile, Sister

Evangelina grumbled her last reprimand, delivered her last baby and was wheeled in her coffin through streets thronged with mourners she had nursed.

Appropriately for a show that puts childbirth centre stage, there is always new life somewhere in *Call the Midwife*. But tears are often shed. Our characters – whether they are beloved regulars, or people we meet and root for only briefly – have to struggle with daily existence in all its messy glory. They might be ill or penniless, lonely or infertile, but somehow we always find a thread of hope or grace for them. For me, despair is the least acceptable of all the human states.

Our fans have always laughed with us, and after every episode Twitter is full of the jokes and bon mots they've enjoyed. The best and the most memorable are included in this book. Quieter, more spiritual reflections, often spoken by the luminous Sister Julienne, are also profoundly popular. We are so often asked questions such as, 'What was it that Sister Monica Joan said about grief when President Kennedy was shot?' and 'Where can I find the words about "belonging" from the end of last week's show?'

Time and again, people write to us about the voice-overs – the short passages of narration that open and close each episode. The tradition began because, as memoirs, the original *Call the Midwife* books were written in the first person. The real Jennifer remained in touch with the nuns who inspired her all her life, and though her words are now written and spoken by others, it feels right for her spirit to stay with us in this way.

Vanessa Redgrave reads these passages so thoughtfully, and with such care, that the lines become more than a sum of their parts. There is comfort in her voice, and strength, and so much wisdom. One way or another, in this fragile world, we need all of these things. We need consolation. We need community, and we need to know that our hopes and fears are heard. Above all else, we need each other. Who are we, and how are we to live, if we don't connect?

This book comes with love from all at *Call the Midwife*, to everyone who has been with us on this journey. Together, we have laughed and cried throughout the best and the worst of times at Nonnatus House, and we will do so in the future. This collection of quotations celebrates our unity. Because, in the words of our narrator: 'What is joy, if it goes unrecorded? And what is love, if it is not shared?'

PART ONE

CALL THE MIDWIFE

MUSINGS ON MIDWIFERY

The word 'midwife' means 'with woman'.
A woman in that situation needs somebody
by her side. Whatever mistakes or choices
brought her to our door.
Sister Julienne *Series 8, Episode 1*

Babies come along when they feel inclined.
We can only prepare; we can never predict.
Mother Mildred *Series 8, Episode 7*

Nothing like manning the gas and air
to start the day.
Trixie *Series 5, Christmas Special*

I had entered a house in the dead of night,
and emerged into sunshine, leaving a new life
behind and I wouldn't have changed my job
for all the world.
Narration by Jennifer *Series 1, Episode 2*

Midwifery is about separation, physically dividing into two that which has been one for nine months. There is beauty and relief in the cleaving. There is labour, but there is reward.
Narration by Jennifer *Series 3, Episode 7*

Ain't you been here long enough yet? We don't have Hollywood endings here, Nurse Miller. We just do our jobs.
Sister Evangelina *Series 2, Episode 7*

I didn't expect glamour when I came into nursing. But I had hoped for something more than a night in discussing square dancing and drinking Horlicks.
Trixie *Series 4, Episode 6*

We are the Sisters of Saint Raymond Nonnatus. Midwives and district nurses, present at life's commencement and at its end.
Sister Monica Joan *Series 1, Episode 1*

Babies are not statistics at
Nonnatus House! We know when
they are wanted or unwanted, whether
they are cherished or deprived.
We see when they're in with a chance
in life, or stand no chance at all.
We value every infant and every
mother, equally. We are part of their
world and they are part of ours.
Because that is what happens when
you enter people's homes!
Trixie *Series 9, Episode 8*

In Nonnatus House, we were good at tending each other's wounds, and there were times when I felt we were all each other's children.
Narration by Jennifer *Series 2, Episode 5*

I think you'll find our patients are more than just a tick at Nonnatus, Dr Walters.
Lucille *Series 9, Episode 4*

We are midwives. We are also nurses, and we're your friends. While we're looking after you, we'll be whichever of those you need most.
Mother Mildred *Series 9, Episode 1*

We don't need an extra pair of hands. We need an octopus.
Sister Evangelina *Series 1, Episode 2*

I may not be on horseback, but consider me the cavalry.
Nurse Crane *Series 5, Episode 7*

I'd like to see a robot trying to do any of our jobs.
Trixie *Series 8, Episode 2*

Don't forget your most essential instruments.
Courage, and humility. If you leaven one with
the other, you cannot fail.
Mother Mildred *Series 8, Episode 7*

Nurse, we're not here to pity! We are here to serve.
Sister Julienne *Series 2, Episode 1*

Gravity can do amazing things.
It keeps our feet on the ground and
brings babies down to earth.
Lucille *Series 7, Episode 1*

Midwifery is the very stuff of life.
Every child is conceived in love, or lust, and born
in pain followed by joy, or by tragedy and
anguish. Every birth is attended by a midwife;
she is in the thick of it. She sees it all.
Narration by Jennifer *Series 1, Episode 1*

> As nurses and midwives, we were adept at silence. We shared much with those we cared for, and saw more than we could ever say.
> **Narration by Jennifer** *Series 2, Episode 6*

Cynthia Yes, and don't you think it might be fun to do things like music and movement with the toddlers?
Sister Evangelina Fun? We're givers of health care. Not children's entertainers! *Series 3, Episode 1*

We're going to welcome a new life into this world. Into a family filled with love. And I need you to do exactly as I tell you. Do you understand?
Sister Winifred *Series 3, Episode 4*

I realise I have to be able to sit with a patient all night if needed, or go to her at a moment's notice. I need to care. I can't ration it or turn it into an efficiency. That'll never be my way.
Jenny *Series 3, Episode 7*

Perhaps stop trying quite so hard and instead just . . . feel. Feel the mother's pain, the mother's joy. The happiness is catching.

Cynthia *Series 3, Episode 4*

We are not machines, and nor are our patients. District practice has variables that preclude such a rigid approach.

Nurse Crane *Series 3, Episode 6*

Nursing isn't easy. That's why there are rules, and systems. Things we can hide in, and behind. Sometimes one simply has to dust off one's brave face and crack on.

Patsy *Series 4, Episode 2*

They were witnesses to all that mattered. Struggle. Loss. Triumph. Ties of blood. Other people's lives were their life. And in their service, they gave all they had. All that they were. They did not stop to count the cost, for this was their mission, their calling, their joy.

Narration by Jennifer *Series 9, Episode 5*

Though we were only in our early twenties, little more than girls, we served the women of the East End in their hour of greatest need. In return for our care, they gave us the most precious gift they could. Their trust. This made us brave and tireless and in the main we did not doubt ourselves because we were not doubted.
Narration by Jennifer *Series 2, Episode 2*

You mark my words;
the joy of midwifery never dims.
Sister Evangelina
Series 4, Episode 6

Kind words are a universal panacea, Sister. Like you, I can dispense them quite liberally when occasion demands. And, like you, I temper them with common sense.
Nurse Crane *Series 5, Episode 1*

To nurse is to be drawn into society,
to interweave one's life with the business
of strangers.
Narration by Jennifer *Series 4, Episode 6*

Shelagh She's made her mark on all of us.
Mother Mildred They do, you know, these little
scraps. They come to us as the wounded ones,
but when they leave us, it is we who bleed.
Series 8, Episode 6

Kevin McNulty What must it be like to have
fifty-six thousand women screaming at you?
Nurse Crane A bad day at a Tuesday clinic,
I should imagine. *Series 9, Episode 6*

It's hardly scientific, but it is full of compassion
and common sense. And much of the time,
that's all a midwife needs.
Sister Evangelina *Series 4, Episode 8*

BEAUTIFUL BIRTH

There are between eighty and one hundred babies born each month in Poplar. As soon as one vacates its pram, another one takes its place! And thus it was and ever shall be, until such time as they invent a magic potion to put a stop to it.
Sister Evangelina *Series 1, Episode 1*

Cynthia Didn't Shakespeare describe Richard III as being breech? Something about him coming into the world with his legs forward?
Sister Monica Joan In Poplar they call it arriving arse first. *Series 1, Episode 2*

The arrival of new life eclipses everything. When all goes well, the room is filled with happiness, and all the pain that went before is forgotten. Where there was mystery there is knowledge. Where there was fear there is love.
Narration by Jennifer *Series 3, Episode 8*

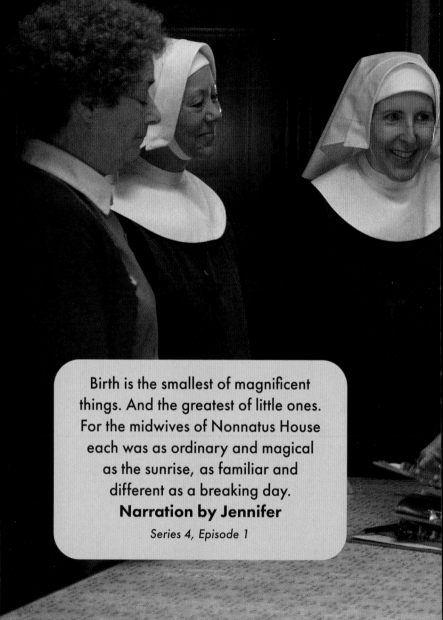

Birth is the smallest of magnificent
things. And the greatest of little ones.
For the midwives of Nonnatus House
each was as ordinary and magical
as the sunrise, as familiar and
different as a breaking day.
Narration by Jennifer
Series 4, Episode 1

When a child is born, the world is altered in an instant. A new voice is heard. New love comes into being. Years later we pause and say, 'Yes, that's when it all began. On that day, in that room. When I saw that face.'
Narration by Jennifer *Series 4, Episode 1*

Mrs Torpy Did I make a cow noise? If I did, it means I'm getting to the sharp end.
Chummy Mrs Torpy. I think we should both remove our hats. *Series 3, Episode 1*

Birth sparked a little light into the gloom, bringing mystery and hope. The unknown, and the longed for, burning like a candle in the night.
Narration by Jennifer *Series 4, Episode 7*

It's a baby, not a lubricated penguin. They don't come sliding out to order!
Sister Evangelina *Series 2, Episode 8*

One can never be sure of everything in childbirth. It doesn't matter whether you are in Poplar or Peking. There may only be so many ways a baby can emerge into the world, but they have a peerless ability to surprise us.
Mother Mildred *Series 8, Episode 7*

Birth is the shortest journey we will ever make. It begins in darkness, and ends – we think – in light. But welcomed, and safe, we rest upon the shore for what amounts to moments, before we begin the greatest voyage of them all. There is no map, no route, no arrowhead to follow. For none of us have ever walked this way before.
Narration by Jennifer *Series 8, Christmas Special*

If you're suggesting that a few deep breaths, and not thinking about what's for dinner is all there is to labour – you're leading your patients up the fairy way.
Sister Evangelina *Series 3, Episode 2*

MOTHERHOOD

Motherhood is about so much more
than a physical process.
Sister Julienne *Series 7, Episode 4*

Oh, love! Oh, what a mess! What a mess.
We'll sort something out, I promise. Because you're
mine. Mine. And I'm not bailing out on you.
Rhoda Mullucks *Series 5, Episode 1*

I can remember my grandmother telling me,
'To feed the baby, one must feed the mother.'
Mumtaz Gani *Series 7, Episode 3*

Every birth begins as a mystery. An enterprise
whose outcome cannot be foretold. We think
'May all be well' and all is well, almost always.
But joy is only the beginning of the journey.
And we must move forward, fuelled by faith.
Narration by Jennifer *Series 8, Episode 3*

Babies can be a shock to the system.
Shelagh *Series 9, Episode 7*

I thought I deserved all manner of medals!
Up all night. Cycling for miles. A wall of wimples
at every single mealtime. And then one day I realised
– I didn't deserve any medals at all. The mothers are
the brave ones. Baby after baby, in abominable
conditions, and they keep on going. They are
the heroines. I'm just here to help.
Trixie *Series 1, Episode 1*

You know, I didn't realise how much my mum loved
me, until I was a mum. It's the kind of love that only
goes one way. Forward. You only realise that when
you have your own. When it's too late to change your
mind. I know what they mean now, when they say
love hurts. You can't have one without the other. Not
ever. Yet we keep on doing it again, and again.
Shirley Redmond *Series 1, Episode 4*

Hard work makes a mother.
We like to think something magical
happens at birth – and for some it
does – but the real magic is keeping
on when all you want to do is run.
Nurse Crane *Series 5, Episode 5*

Bringing up children is not
simple. From the moment the
midwife cuts the cord, a mother's
task is to nurture and cherish, to
shelter and protect. Even as she
does so, she must teach the child
to leave her. Train it to let go of
her hand – first, to walk unaided
and then to walk away. But there
is a cord that nothing can sever.
The invisible bond that ties the
mother to her infant, which
endures when the child is a
child no more.
Narration by Jennifer
Series 6, Episode 5

THE FEMALE BODY

Our bodies are only part of who we are.
Trixie *Series 8, Episode 5*

Trixie There are women in my group who can't
even name parts of their own anatomy! They expect
to be in discomfort – even pain – because they
haven't been taught that owning a female body
ought to be a joy!
Sister Julienne But it so often isn't, Nurse Franklin.
That's what our work is about.
Trixie And it shouldn't have to be!
Series 5, Episode 1

There is a time to mortify our flesh.
And a time to cherish it, and marvel at its strength.
Sister Monica Joan *Series 5, Episode 6*

So the workings of this automobile are not unlike the workings of the human body. It requires fuel to power it, a heart to keep it running, lights to shine the way, and a system that prevents overheating.
Sister Monica Joan *Series 8, Episode 5*

Every woman alive is the sum of all she ever did, and felt, and was.
Sister Julienne *Series 6, Episode 8*

The female body is a complex thing; at once fragile and formidable, vulnerable and brave. It carries the seed of our hopes, the bloom of our youth, the weight of our fears. It can nurture and tremble, inspire and terrify. It oppresses and protects us, holding within it all that we are, projecting less than we wish to be. It is our enemy, our friend. The very vessel of our being.
Narration by Jennifer *Series 5, Episode 1*

THE HEALTH SERVICE

Being a doctor isn't just about handing out pills.
Dr Turner *Series 9, Episode 7*

No doctor, and no nurse, should ever tell
a patient there is nothing they can do!
Lucille *Series 8, Episode 8*

Somewhere in all the notes – or lack of
them – we lose sight of the patient.
Nurse Crane *Series 9, Episode 3*

Exactly what the National Health should stand for.
Good people doing good work.
Dr Latham *Series 3, Episode 2*

Nursing is about curing patients, Trixie.
Not our own broken hearts.
Nurse Crane *Series 7, Episode 4*

Dr Turner The world is full of fragile people, Kevin.
And when we try to mend them, it can break us.
Kevin McNulty Have you ever been broken?
Dr Turner Yes. And I became a better doctor.

Series 9, Episode 8

I've never quite got used to it, as a nurse.
The way you can suddenly see yourself reflected
back at you. In a place, or a face,
where you least expect it.
Trixie *Series 9, Christmas Special*

Good doctors never jump to conclusions.
But they can reach for them. And they can be led.
Dr Turner *Series 9, Episode 4*

To change the world one lives in, one must start with where one lives!
Nurse Crane
Series 8, Episode 2

PART TWO

LOVE AND FAMILY

WORDS OF LOVE

I am nothing if not an incurable romantic.
Tom *Series 5, Episode 6*

People want what they want.
And one way or another – at least, if love comes
into it – things will end up as they should.
Trixie *Series 5, Episode 4*

We must see what love can do.
Sister Julienne *Series 1, Episode 1*

Love permeated every nook and cranny,
every corner and crevice of that little house.
You could feel it as soon as you entered the
front door. A presence so tangible you
could reach out and touch it.
Narration by Jennifer *Series 1, Episode 5*

I had begun to see what love could do.
Love brought life into the world, and women
to their knees. Love had the power to
break hearts, and to save.
Narration by Jennifer *Series 1, Episode 1*

If I never said I was grateful to you, I say it now.
If I never said I was proud of the home that you kept,
I say it now. If I didn't tell you that you were beautiful
when your face grew lined, when you didn't have a
new blouse from one summer's end to the next,
I say it now. And if I didn't you tell that I loved you,
I say it now. Missing you, I will talk about tomorrow.
Arnold Gelin *Series 7, Episode 1*

I find the exuberance of young love a joy to behold,
and essential for the progression of the human race.
Sister Monica Joan *Series 9, Episode 4*

Love is never the only answer.
But it is always the best,
the simplest, the one most likely
to withstand the test of time.
Love is the beginning.
It should be the final word.
Narration by Jennifer
Series 8, Episode 4

I never know when I love you the most.
But I sometimes think that these are the times that
I love you best. When the whole world's sleeping,
and you're sitting up with dark rings beneath
your eyes, just trying to make it better.
Shelagh *Series 5, Episode 4*

One doesn't choose whom one falls in love with.
Trixie *Series 8, Episode 2*

Love cannot always save us.
But it can be the reason why we fight.
Narration by Jennifer *Series 7, Episode 7*

That day we got married, and I was all wrapped
up in my cloak, that was the safest I've ever felt.
And that's because of you, Tom.
Barbara *Series 7, Episode 7*

Hold each other close. Keep each other safe.
For there is imperfection everywhere.
There are always wounds that weep.
Narration by Jennifer *Series 7, Christmas Special*

Chummy I'm turning myself in. I am guilty of criminal cowardice, and of robbing two people of something that would make them both very happy. I have decided it's time to be brave.
PC Noakes I see.
Chummy I hope so. Because underneath this raincoat, I am practically naked.
Series 1, Episode 6

Fear can keep us tethered. Terror can clip our wings. But trust eases pain. Hope can lighten the sky. Love makes us courageous.
Narration by Jennifer *Series 7, Episode 5*

Humanity is fragile, and all the sunshine in the world can't save the frail, or make the delicate invincible. But love has the power to strengthen, and protect, and guide us to a place where we feel sheltered and fulfilled. Where it doesn't matter if it rains, for we are home and dry.
Narration by Jennifer
Series 4, Episode 5

Love doesn't seem to adhere to time or boundaries, does it? It just is.
Cynthia *Series 1, Episode 4*

There is nothing wrong with being romantic.
Dr Turner *Series 3, Episode 3*

Barbara. I want you to have this. No hand has ever touched it but mine, and it's as though it has been growing here, just waiting for this moment. There'll be a gold ring. There'll be a diamond if you want one. But for now, you beautiful girl, will you just let me love you, and accept this blade of grass?

Tom

Series 6, Christmas Special

Love cannot ease every anguish in the world.
But tenderly applied, it can transfigure fortunes,
light up faces. Turn the tide.
Narration by Jennifer *Series 2, Episode 1*

You've been disappointed in love. It doesn't
mean there wasn't love there to begin with.
Nurse Crane *Series 9, Episode 2*

There'll be plenty of time for romance when
I'm older. Now how about some more of
those biscuits?
Jenny *Series 1, Episode 3*

So much can be made bearable by love.
By cherishing what is, and not condemning fault
or flaw. By never locking doors, by keeping
hearts open, and holding each other forever
in the light.
Narration by Jennifer *Series 5, Episode 3*

Health is the greatest of God's gifts, but we take it for granted. Yet it hangs on a thread as fine as a spider's web, and the tiniest thing can make it snap, leaving the strongest of us helpless in an instant. And in that instant, hope is our protector, and love our panacea.
Narration by Jennifer *Series 1, Episode 5*

I think we all know more about love than we might realise.
Dr Turner *Series 7, Episode 4*

I know love has dealt you a blow, or two. But I really don't think you ought to throw your entire life on the pyre.
Trixie *Series 1, Episode 5*

Some of us are not blessed with revelations or confessions. Love cannot be spoken, only shown.
Narration by Jennifer *Series 2, Episode 6*

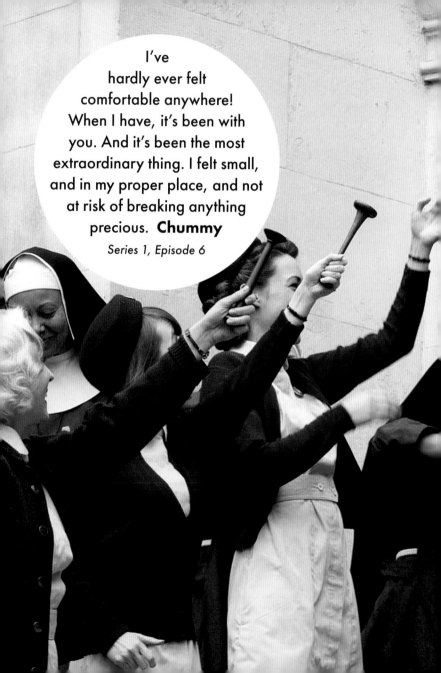

I've hardly ever felt comfortable anywhere! When I have, it's been with you. And it's been the most extraordinary thing. I felt small, and in my proper place, and not at risk of breaking anything precious. **Chummy**

Series 1, Episode 6

If there's one thing the religious life has taught me, is it's impossible to love too much. What's needed is taken up, and what's not needed hangs around somewhere, looking for a home.

Sister Evangelina *Series 3, Episode 5*

Lady Browne One cannot survive on love.
Chummy One cannot survive without it.

Series 3, Episode 7

Tom Please be advised I had every intention of kissing you when we first met.
Trixie And I had every intention of letting you.
Trixie takes something out of the pocket of her raincoat.
Trixie Scotch egg?
Tom You're like a sort of angel sometimes.

Series 4, Episode 1

Tom If I could rub all that out for you, I would. If I could take every scrap of unhappiness you've ever had away, I would.

Trixie And you can't. But just standing here, with you, hearing you say that reminds me that I've survived it. And that others might not, if we don't help. *Series 4, Episode 1*

Violet I believe in the films they say, 'Your place or mine?'

Fred I'd live in a ditch if it was with you.

Series 4, Episode 8

We get so much out of love. We find strength in it, and courage. Love is our foundation, and our fuel. But if we don't show enough of it then we might as well not feel any love at all.

Sister Julienne *Series 5, Christmas Special*

Fred Violet. Would you be averse to me paying you a compliment?

Violet So long as it doesn't interfere with my press-stud inventory.

Fred You have got a lovely silhouette.

Violet Don't you start talking to me in French, Fred Buckle. You don't know where it might end.

Series 6, Episode 1

I'd come to a meeting of the WI,
if you were going to be there.
Alec *Series 3, Episode 3*

Nadine Mulvaney I let her in, Nurse. I let her in,
and it was like she tore me open! Not just my body,
but my whole self. I'm not sure I even knew I had
a whole self, until she came.
Trixie Some people spend a lifetime
waiting for love like that.
Nadine Mulvaney And some people are just
scared of it.
Series 7, Episode 1

THE IMPORTANCE OF FRIENDSHIP

Life was fuelled by learning, but there was laughter too. And I was forging friendships that would last me all my days.
Narration by Jennifer *Series 2, Episode 1*

Nurse Crane Right, lad. You and I are good pals, and if there's one thing neither of us like, it's a lot of fussing and fretting.
Reggie That's two things. *Series 7, Episode 5*

It is no matter if we meet as strangers, for we can join forces and learn to love. And where there is friendship, and affection, there is the place we can all call home.
Narration by Jennifer *Series 6, Episode 3*

Let friendship flourish, and let love in. So it might feed and sustain us all our days.
Narration by Jennifer

Series 3, Episode 6

She had friends around her, but had not yet had time to make their acquaintance. Friends are everywhere, if one has the eyes to see them.
Sister Monica Joan

Series 8, Episode 2

When a secret weighs heavy, we imagine it is our burden alone, but the opposite is true. Once it is spoken, it disappears.
Sister Monica Joan

Series 9, Episode 7

Sometimes one small gesture can give us
the strength to do enormous things. A little
generosity can unleash great tenderness,
leading in time to deep, real love. And a single
conversation can change a mind, a life.
The world is no bigger than the people who
inhabit it. And together, or alone, we are closer
than we know.
Narration by Jennifer *Series 7, Episode 4*

I know that fun doesn't come in bottles now.
I know the value of sobriety. And I know what
friendship really is, what it means.
I always did, I just couldn't see it.
Trixie *Series 5, Episode 7*

There are no devils here. Your mind gets tired,
Sister, that is all. And when it does, we will protect
you. We will be with you, and make sure that
when you forget, we remember.
Sister Julienne *Series 2, Episode 7*

Sister Evangelina used to say that the best medicine
for pain was the presence of another person.
Shelagh *Series 7, Episode 8*

Barbara And what I want to ask you is this, Phyllis.
Will you be my bridesmaid?
Nurse Crane Your . . . your bridesmaid?
Oh, no, Barbara. No. You ought to
choose one of your friends.
Barbara I have chosen one of my friends. I've
chosen you! We've been sharing a bedroom for two
years, Phyllis. Going halves on the mantelpiece, and
the bedside table. And taking it in turns to open the
curtains and turn the light off. And if I snore, you've
never once complained or even mentioned it.
Nurse Crane You hardly do it on purpose.
Barbara You've taught me as much about living
alongside another person as anyone else in my life,
Phyllis. And I'm ready to move on, and share
everything I have with someone who is unbelievably
dear to me. And that's because you've been the
very best friend I could have had. *Series 6, Episode 8*

FAMILY VALUES

Dr Turner Tim. Whatever happens with
this baby, family life won't change.
Timothy But I'll change.
Dr Turner You've been changing for fifteen
years. And I love you just the same.
Series 6, Episode 4

It's a funny old fandangle, family. Sometimes,
I'm telling you, it's like trying to plait soot.
Dolly, Fred's daughter *Series 2, Episode 8*

Home is not simply a mark upon a map, any
more than a river is just water. It is the place at
the centre of the compass from which every
arrow radiates, and where the heart is fixed. It is
a force that forever draws us back or lures us on.
For where the home is, there lies hope.
Narration by Jennifer *Series 2, Episode 7*

So where, in the end, do we belong?
In the eyes of another, where we see ourselves
reflected? Or arm in arm with those whose faces
echo ours, whose blood we share? Or is it in the
heart of the family we create, where we are
safest, and best known, and never lonely?
Perhaps we belong where love can bloom,
because we give it room to put down roots,
and space in which to thrive. Seeds fly in upon
the wind, and settle where they will.
We all belong somewhere.
Narration by Jennifer *Series 8, Episode 6*

I grew up in my bare feet. My dad spent more
on beer than he did on shoe leather. I used to think,
when I have kids, I'm going give them shoes,
hot dinners, a happy home. And I managed all three,
until Hitler intervened. When the bomb dropped,
I weren't there. And that's what makes you a parent,
Nurse Noakes. Proximity. They don't sell
that in the shops.
Fred *Series 2, Episode 8*

What is a family? Is it just the tie of flesh and blood? Our facial features, and the traits we inherit, and pass on? Or is it the rhythm our hearts beat out, marking out the days we share? Family is our touchstone, our haven. Family is the place where life begins.

Narration by Jennifer *Series 7, Episode 3*

A world is not just made of bricks and mortar, but of minds. We can rebuild cities, paint beautiful façades, invent new ways of living. We can protect all that we have. But that place which we call home must be the place in which we are ourselves. With no façade, no foundations weak below us. Only then can we face outwards with our heads held high, playing the roles assigned to us with open, honest hearts.
Narration by Jennifer *Series 4, Episode 3*

Nurse Crane It can be a hard thing when a child must become the carer to a parent.
Sister Monica Joan But surely it is no more than we owe? A repayment for all the care, and sacrifices, they themselves have expended on us.
Series 9, Episode 2

And it's like when I was a kid, and I bunked in with my brothers. And that's what family meant. It meant no space. No silence. No being lonely in the dark.
Dena Bowland *Series 9, Episode 1*

KINDNESS AND UNDERSTANDING

I have come to the conclusion that there
are only two reasons for ever doing anything.
One is love, and the other is fear.
Sister Julienne *Series 2, Christmas Special*

What the poor pet really needs is a good cry,
a couple of aspirin, and a hug. In no particular
order, but the hug is of prime importance.
Trixie *Series 5, Episode 4*

It doesn't matter where any of us are from, or
where we go, as long as we hold on to one another.
Tom *Series 7, Christmas Special*

No one ever gets in trouble for being kind, Reggie.
Dr Turner *Series 7, Episode 5*

At times of great happiness, Nurse Gilbert,
it is sometimes as well to remember that others
may be ploughing a less congenial path.
Sister Julienne *Series 6, Episode 8*

Listen attentively. Reassure gently. Love generously.
Dr Turner
Series 8, Episode 1

DR. TURNER

Isla MacLeod He knows I'm hurt. I can see it in his eyes.
Trixie That's all we can hope for really, isn't it? Someone who knows when we're in pain.
Series 9, Christmas Special

Sometimes we have to wait for our help to be asked for.
Sister Mary Cynthia
Series 4, Episode 7

Where would I be, if not alongside you? You were born into our hands, your trials are ours.
Sister Julienne *Series 8, Episode 8*

Love cannot ease every anguish in the world, but tenderly applied, it can transfigure fortunes, light up faces. Turn the tide.
Narration by Jennifer *Series 2, Episode 1*

BELONGING

This is home now. Wherever I went,
I'd wing my way back here like a bally racing
pigeon. Home. Heart is. All of that.
Chummy *Series 2, Episode 1*

It's a very great gift in life, to know
where you belong. Many spend a lifetime
hoping to find out.
Sister Julienne *Series 9, Christmas Special*

Fate might shake us, but our roots run deep,
and we have love to water them.
And so we bloom where we are planted.
Turning our faces to the sun.
Narration by Jennifer *Series 3, Christmas Special*

CHILDREN

I find infant charms somewhat exaggerated.
So uninspiring until they can converse. He may
yet inherit some of my father's talent for politics.
Goodness knows the country's in need of
a decent politician.
Lady Browne *Series 3, Episode 7*

Children are alert to any joy that comes their way.
Any smile that's tossed in their direction.
Some of us carry that with us all our lives.
Trixie *Series 9, Episode 1*

Children must be loved.
There is no rule of life so simple, or so true.
Narration by Jennifer *Series 6, Episode 7*

Sister Monica Joan When do you suppose babies became so very precious?
Cynthia What do you mean, Sister Monica Joan?
Sister Monica Joan Well once, they played naked in gutters, or balanced on the hips of siblings scarcely older than themselves. Are they more valued now because they can survive, or do they survive because they are more valued?

Series 2, Episode 5

COMMUNITY

I know it seems like small potatoes, but it's the little things that make a community. It used to be that folk that lived round here had family to rely on, but Poplar's changing. Old families are moving out, fresh ones are moving in. I want to make Poplar a place that feels like home to all her residents – old and new. That's how we'll build a community that can thrive, and expand, and be rich in opportunity for all.

Violet *Series 8, Episode 2*

We have always helped our neighbours where we can. And the people in this district are our neighbours, not objects of charity or pity.

Sister Julienne *Series 6, Episode 2*

Sometimes it is easier to talk to strangers than our loved ones.

Trixie *Series 8, Episode 5*

However great the scale of injury or loss, our frailties and pains are made bearable by others – their thoughts, their deeds, their reaching out. Their love, and our endurance, make us human, and complete.
Narration by Jennifer *Series 6, Episode 2*

Inspector So why do you think they chose to come to you?
Dr Turner Because they want to stay in the community. They want the midwives who saw them through their pregnancy, and they want their families close at hand. Without the Maternity Home, many of our patients would have the choice between giving birth in damp, overcrowded housing, or a bus ride, while in labour, to a hospital where their children couldn't visit. Personally, I don't think that's any choice at all.
Series 6, Episode 3

Fred You ever felt like you've bitten
off more than you can chew, Sister?
Sister Hilda Ha! Quite frequently. I usually find
that spreading the load around a bit is the answer.
Series 9, Episode 6

A small amount of change is good for a
community. Too much isn't.
Sister Julienne *Series 4, Episode 8*

Light will often pierce the darkness when
we least expect it. And if we're fortunate,
when we need it most, science can pave the way.
But we need human hands to guide us, and love
to illuminate the path that lies ahead.
Narration by Jennifer *Series 4, Episode 7*

All islands are like this. All islands have a boundary, and you live your life within it, and you love it, or you break out, and make a life elsewhere. And on every island in the world, no matter how magnificent, there are those who cannot leave, and those who cannot stay.

Lucille *Series 9, Christmas Special*

Sometimes, the route to joy is indirect, our journey home not quite as we expected. There is no magic star to guide our steps, no ancient prophecies to predict our way. The greatest gift is to know that we travel not alone, but in the company of others. That there are hands we can reach for, and hearts to keep us warm.

Narration by Jennifer *Series 5, Christmas Special*

PART THREE

HARD TIMES

FAITH

I thought at first that it was a test of faith, but it was only a test of strength. I can bear more than I ever thought I could. And I can bear it for others, because my strength is a gift from Him.
Sister Mary Cynthia *Series 5, Episode 6*

Belief is the beginning of all things.
Narration by Jennifer *Series 9, Episode 7*

Fred People are trying to help you. You're rejecting that. Medical science can help you. You're rejecting that too. And if you believe that God created the world, then He made all of those things possible! And I would be a little bit fed up with you, if I was the man upstairs.
Sister Monica Joan The man upstairs knows my reasoning.
Fred In which case, He also knows you're scared. *Series 6, Episode 4*

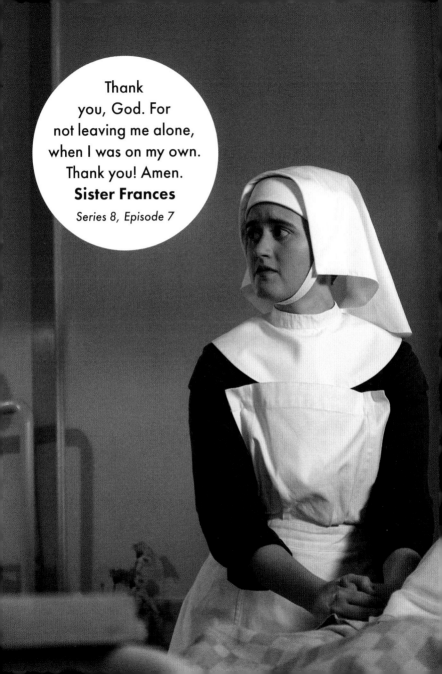

Thank you, God. For not leaving me alone, when I was on my own. Thank you! Amen.
Sister Frances
Series 8, Episode 7

I wasn't entirely sure what I should make of it.
I was young, and faith was still a mystery to me.
Narration by Jennifer *Series 2, Christmas Special*

The way you worship is your own affair.
We wear the habit, you wear your uniform.
But we are all nurses first, and midwives foremost.
Sister Julienne *Series 1, Episode 1*

I need your strength, Sister. I don't have enough
of my own. Because I don't know if God's given me
a window, and I'm just staring out of it because
I'm afraid to open it?
Sister Bernadette *Series 2, Episode 7*

Sister Bernadette Who is it who decides
what is forgivable, and unforgivable?
Dr Turner I think you know that better than I do.
Sister Bernadette At this moment, I only know . . .
that I am not turning my back on you because of you.
I am doing it because of Him.
Dr Turner And if I didn't accept that,
I wouldn't deserve to live. *Series 2, Episode 5*

We are none of us cast adrift, if we have faith.
In the cross, we find our anchor.
Sister Monica Joan *Series 7, Episode 5*

The hands of the Almighty are so often
to be found at the ends of our own arms.
Sister Monica Joan *Series 7, Christmas Special*

God isn't in the event. He is in the response
to the event. In the love that is shown,
and the care that is given.
Sister Julienne *Series 3, Episode 4*

I've always found that by trusting in God,
nothing is inevitable.
Tom *Series 6, Episode 2*

In later life, I came to see that faith, like hope,
is a rope and anchor in a shifting world.
Faith cannot be questioned, only lived. And if
I could not grasp it then, I felt its heartbeat.
Which was love.
Narration by Jennifer *Series 2, Christmas Special*

If I may venture an observation,
when people seek the approval of
the Almighty, it is generally because
they fear they will not get it.
Sister Monica Joan
Series 6, Episode 4

When I first joined The Order,
the Postulant Mistress used to say,
'When a prayer is answered,
don't send a question back.'
Sister Julienne
Series 4, Episode 2

If fifty years
in the religious life
has taught me anything,
it's that miracles are in very
short supply. We had better
not rely on them.
Mother Mildred
Series 8, Episode 6

I saw faith growing in you,
like some flower whose name I'd never know.
Charles Newgarden *Series 4, Episode 2*

Sister Julienne Prayers aren't always
answered the way one would hope, but . . .
Sister Evangelina They are generally answered.
Series 5, Episode 7

The Lord has given you a voice. And if
you are called, He will give you the courage.
Lucille *Series 9, Episode 3*

The Almighty likes to keep us guessing.
It is why my devotion to Him never stales.
Mother Mildred *Series 8, Episode 6*

Well, it must be wonderful to be so saintly.
Personally, I always think those who've struggled
with temptation are far more interesting.
Trixie *Series 9, Episode 2*

Sister. It is best if we remain within convenient distance of the altar rail. By the time I inform you of my plan, we might both feel the need to pray.

Mother Mildred *Series 9, Christmas Special*

When I was a novice, I found Lent the hardest season. Not for the hardship of self-sacrifice – that I willingly embraced – but for the absence of nature's beauty in the chapel. I always found it an invaluable aid to spiritual labour. But then I encountered a passage that gave great illumination. It is not the penance that we choose that is pleasing to God – it is the setting aside of ego and the submission to His will.

Sister Monica Joan *Series 9, Episode 2*

COURAGE

We have a duty to live every moment the
best we can. I mean really live it. Even if it means
getting hurt. Otherwise what's the point?
We mustn't let fear stop us.
Cynthia *Series 1, Episode 4*

You're succeeding just by putting one foot in
front of the other, carrying on along this scary,
rocky, lonely road.
Dr Turner *Series 6, Episode 6*

You have to be brave to be in love, don't you?
I mean, knowing that your heart may get broken
at some point along the way.
Cynthia *Series 1, Episode 4*

Sometimes, never letting go becomes a
letting in, an opening up. And surrender itself
can be the bravest act of all.
Narration by Jennifer *Series 8, Episode 2*

It is not always sunshine that splits the seed, cleaving the armour, releasing the shoot. Darkness makes the heart's case fragile. Pain breaks it open. Courage teases out the leaves, and life unfurls and expands, thrusting upwards into light.
Narration by Jennifer *Series 7, Episode 1*

The quarrel is not between ourselves, but within us. The quarrel is between our own desire, and that which is demanded. The quarrel is between the body, and its longings, the soul and its terrors, the mind and its yearning to be free. The quarrel defines us. It drives us. Forward, upward, to our knees in prayer. You must embrace the quarrel. The quarrel will lead us to the answer. It is everything we are.
Mother Mildred *Series 9, Christmas Special*

Chummy Gosh. Courage. I wish we could bottle it, like gas and air.
Jenny Sister Evangelina wouldn't approve.
Series 2, Episode 1

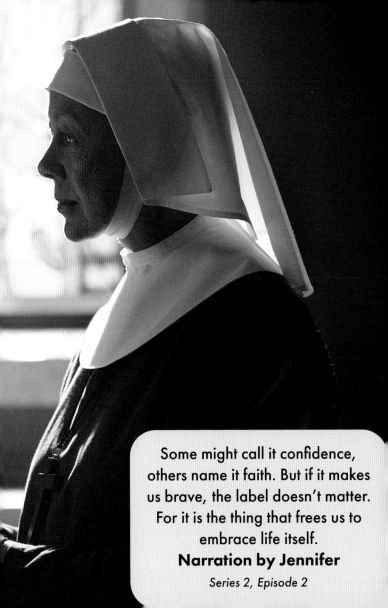

Some might call it confidence, others name it faith. But if it makes us brave, the label doesn't matter. For it is the thing that frees us to embrace life itself.
Narration by Jennifer

Series 2, Episode 2

Sometimes love is not enough.
Courage is worth more.
And common sense, more still.
Sister Mildred *Series 8, Christmas Special*

Jeannie, we never know
what we can achieve, until we try.
Trixie *Series 8, Episode 4*

Dr Turner Well done. You learn to keep
that sigh in, over time.
Kevin McNulty Does it get easier?
Dr Turner It gets easier to hide. Usually.
Series 9, Episode 6

Sometimes we have to stop wondering and worrying,
and we simply have to do what scares us most.
Patsy *Series 6, Episode 2*

Courage cannot move mountains.
But it can show us how to climb, find a way,
forge a path that we believe in.
Narration by Jennifer *Series 8, Episode 2*

Failure isn't fatal. But hesitation can be.
Give yourself a chance.
Nurse Crane *Series 6, Episode 6*

I think you're being compassionate, sensible,
and bold in equal measure. There can be no
better way to start any enterprise.
Sister Julienne *Series 4, Episode 1*

Staying sober is about not giving in, not letting
go, not allowing yourself to do the one thing that
will make you happy. Self-discipline becomes a habit.
Self-protection becomes a habit. And you think you're
putting on armour, but in truth you're building a cage.
And it's safe in a cage. You can even sing quite a
satisfactory song, as I've discovered. But one
way or another, you're still behind bars.
You just aren't having anything to drink.
Trixie *Series 7, Episode 1*

Fear is never 'just' fear, though, is it, Phyllis?
Trixie *Series 8, Episode 1*

LOSS

I'm good at my job, very good at it. I know how to look after my patients. All of this – Nonnatus, Poplar. Terribly good at all of it. But losing someone? Nope. Not good at that at all.

Patsy *Series 6, Episode 2*

Flowers take many forms. Each one has its story, and its roots. Each one unfurls from its bulb, or its kernel, revealing itself and all its promise, as it will. Each is entirely precious, and unique. Each is the best, and the only. Each will linger in the mind, each will teach us what it is to love, to be torn, to nurture and let go. But not every garden blooms as we expected. Despite our care, not every child can thrive. Tears take the place of rain, and the sunshine fails us. But the buds, however delicate, were precious. They were real. And their fleeting scent will live forever on the air.

Narration by Jennifer *Series 9, Episode 6*

The seasons will always turn. The clouds will gather, and the cold will come. We will survive them. We will grow, regardless of the weather. We will know wonder, where there has been despair. There will be happiness, and we will remember it. There will be friendships, which we won't forget. Love is the constant, whereby we endure all winters, and all storms. It is the climate in which all things can thrive. Welcome the darkness. Embrace it as a canopy, from which the stars can hang. For there are always stars, when we are where we ought to be, amongst the faces we love best. Each with our place, each with our purpose, as fixed and familiar as the constellations. The darkness is beautiful. For how else can we shine?

Narration by Jennifer *Series 9, Episode 8*

I've never found grief and a cold spread to be an easy combination.

Nurse Crane *Series 7, Episode 8*

Sometimes, when a terrible thing happens,
and we survive it, we find something beautiful
waiting for us on the other side.
Trixie *Series 7, Christmas Special*

Sometimes life is shattered in an instant.
And all our certainties are savagely
stripped away.
Narration by Jennifer *Series 7, Episode 7*

We are not what we have lost! We are not what
has been taken from us. You are all too willing to
embrace the void. If you do not cherish what remains,
you will all become as nothing. You will be nothing.
We are not broken. We are each as whole as we
will ever be again. And in the end, when we cease
to be, we will all become memories!
Sister Monica Joan *Series 7, Episode 8*

When people have no love to live for,
it's so very easy to fill that void with hate.
Dr Myra *Series 6, Christmas Special*

A dying person needs to have someone with them, to hold their hand, stroke their forehead, whisper a few words.
Narration by Jennifer *Series 1, Episode 5*

But I feel so much sorrow.
I feel it every time a child is lost, every time a mother is lost. I feel it every time I see somebody weeping. Even if they don't allow the tears to fall.
Sister Julienne *Series 6, Christmas Special*

No one can go through life without experiencing any pain at all.
Fred *Series 8, Episode 8*

The departure of life eclipses everything. When a death is good, the room is filled with peace, and all the pain that went before it is forgotten. Where there was mystery, there is knowledge, where there was fear, there is love.
Narration by Jennifer *Series 3, Episode 8*

97

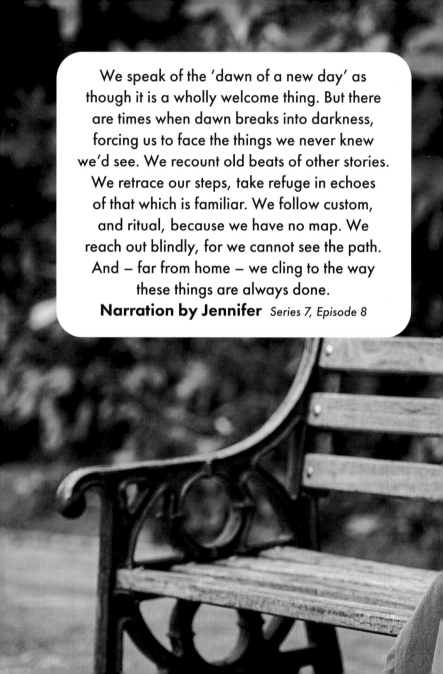

We speak of the 'dawn of a new day' as though it is a wholly welcome thing. But there are times when dawn breaks into darkness, forcing us to face the things we never knew we'd see. We recount old beats of other stories. We retrace our steps, take refuge in echoes of that which is familiar. We follow custom, and ritual, because we have no map. We reach out blindly, for we cannot see the path. And – far from home – we cling to the way these things are always done.

Narration by Jennifer *Series 7, Episode 8*

We flicker on a screen, we fold and unfold upon the mind's eye, brittle as wings, eternal as a heartbeat. And even when the heart falls silent, we do not cease to be. Because — in the end — we all become memories.
Narration by Jennifer *Series 7, Episode 8*

Mrs Rubin You will feel better than this, bubelah. Maybe not yet. But you will.
Jenny Will I?
Mrs Rubin Yes. You just keep living. Until you're alive again. *Series 3, Episode 4*

The world is full of love that goes unspoken. It doesn't mean that it is felt less deeply, or that separation leaves a cleaner wound. Its beauty and its pain are in its silence.
Narration by Jennifer *Series 2, Episode 6*

Some people need permission to die, from those that they love the most.
Cynthia *Series 1, Episode 4*

If I may quote a poem: 'For love of you,
the air, it hurts, and my heart, and my hat,
they hurt me. Who would buy it from me, this
ribbon I am holding, and this sadness of cotton,
white, for making handkerchiefs with? Ay, the pain
it costs me to love you as I love you.' Not my words,
but those of García Lorca. I'm not one for Spanish
poetry – give me Tennyson any day – but I find his
words move me. I have a volume of his poems – in
English – if you should care to borrow it?
And, if I may: 'the pain it costs' to love,
I believe it is always worth it.
Nurse Crane *Series 6, Episode 2*

There are ties that endure for a lifetime,
no matter how frayed by fate. We can walk
away, and pretend that we forget them. Pain
passes in the end. Or we can step into the future,
blessed, and stronger than before. Because,
when faced with change, our love held
fast and did not break.
Narration by Jennifer *Series 2, Episode 3*

It's funny what people take with them when they go. And what they bring back.
Fred *Series 9, Episode 1*

Waiting for a passing is like waiting for a birth. We need things to keep us occupied.
Nurse Crane *Series 7, Episode 1*

One does not have to be a child to be an orphan.
Mother Mildred *Series 9, Episode 1*

Not all of us will choose what we give up. The things we love are taken, or were never ours at all. If we are lucky, life is defined not by what we let go, but what we let in.
Narration by Jennifer *Series 9, Episode 2*

ACCEPTANCE

There is a part of me that you cannot see. But she can. And if she is loved, then I can go on living.
Jacob Milligan *Series 3, Episode 5*

What cannot be changed must be endured.
Sister Monica Joan *Series 7, Episode 2*

Self-doubt is a very good seedbed for progress. And humility, the perfect fertiliser.
Mother Mildred *Series 8, Episode 1*

The thing that matters is never the thing itself, but rather, what we make of it. What we do with our patience, and our imagination. What we allow to thrive. Nothing is ever beyond repair. We break, we bleed, and we begin again. Trust can be mended. Love can be restored. New shoots can flourish, among the broken stones.
Narration by Jennifer *Series 9, Episode 3*

Perhaps, most of all, we are what we accept. What we allow to be important, what we embrace about each other and ourselves. There is nothing better. There is nothing more hopeful. There is nothing else.

Narration by Jennifer *Series 8, Episode 5*

We can decide to be happy. Make much out of little, embrace the warmth of our ordinary days. Life unfolds, as a mystery. An enterprise whose outcome cannot be foretold. We do not get what we expect. We stumble on cracks, are faced with imperfection. Bonds are tested, and tightened. And our landscapes shift, in sunshine and in shade. There is light. There is. Look for it. Look for it shining over your shoulder, on the past. It was light where you went once. It is light where you are now. It will be light, where you will go again.

Narration by Jennifer *Series 8, Episode 3*

Our deepest desires are never simple. But the peace we find when they are met eclipses everything. Rhythm restored, a familiar face returned, the fresh new ticking of a clock once stopped. When wishes are granted, joy comes gently. And when it is not, we hang suspended, waiting for release in the space between the heartbeats.
Narration by Jennifer *Series 6, Episode 4*

I do not believe in weeds. Look at that glorious colour! A weed is simply a flower that someone decides is in the wrong place.
Sister Monica Joan *Series 5, Episode 3*

This is the way the world works – a toss of a coin deciding whether you get what you want, or what you deserve.
Elsie *Series 8, Episode 8*

Sister Monica Joan We are all God's creatures.
Barbara It's just some are easier to love than others.
Sister Monica Joan It is the others that need us most.
Series 4, Episode 3

I think in
all my talk of
duty, perhaps I
forgot to speak of joy.
Patsy
Series 6, Episode 2

Sister Monica Joan The world would be a far more harmonious place were we less concerned with the imagined strengths and frailty of others.
Sister Julienne If we weren't alert to the frailties of others, there is a great deal of caring that wouldn't get done. *Series 7, Episode 4*

The rest will unfold as it unfolds.
Lucille *Series 7, Episode 1*

The heavens don't always protect us. They choose, on occasion, to throw down challenges instead of simply showering more blessings on our heads. Not every tempest passes in an instant. Not every deluge can be brushed off. We can cower. We can wait for blue skies to be restored, or we can take the plunge, defy the elements. And we can seize the day.
Narration by Jennifer *Series 9, Episode 4*

Sometimes the heart desires such very simple things. The heart holds within it all that is most precious, all that we must protect. It is also braver and bolder, more resilient than we realise. If we wound it, it will heal. And if it breaks, it learns to beat again.
Narration by Jennifer *Series 6, Episode 4*

It is no bad thing to be lost in a fog, all at sea. When land comes into view again, you will appreciate it with a keenness that is denied to those who know nothing but the safety of the shore.
Sister Monica Joan *Series 6, Episode 6*

Joy is not felt less exquisitely because the moment flies. And if we can taste it, we know that we are blessed.
Narration by Jennifer *Series 4, Episode 1*

PERFECTION

I find two opinions are always better than one.
Particularly if one is mine.
Sister Monica Joan *Series 6, Episode 5*

We only fail when we do not try.
Sister Monica Joan *Series 6, Episode 2*

Perfection is not a polished thing. It is often
simply something that is sincerely meant.
Perfection is a job complete, praise given, prayer
heard. It can be kindness shown, thanks offered
up. Perfection is what we discover in each other,
what we see reflected back.
Narration by Jennifer *Series 3, Episode 5*

To be human is to be imperfect,
and to accept that is to thrive.
Narration by Jennifer *Series 9, Episode 2*

> The soul, being stronger than we think,
> can survive all mutilations. And the marks upon
> it make it perfect and complete.
> **Narration by Jennifer** *Series 6, Episode 6*

TOLERANCE

People who have secrets, they're usually afraid.
Afraid of being laughed at, or rejected, or punished.
Persecuted even. Nobody does it for fun, I promise you.
Valerie *Series 6, Episode 7*

The Beatles do seem a bit . . . nicer than
the Rolling Stones.
Shelagh *Series 8, Episode 5*

All I would say is, speaking entirely from my own
experience, is that when somebody thinks the worst
of a person because of their background . . .
such a lot can be lost.
Nurse Crane *Series 4, Episode 6*

Anyone saying anything sideways deserves to be corrected. The National Health was struggling, till all these girls started coming from the Commonwealth.
Nurse Crane
Series 7, Episode 1

HOPE

I'm not one for biblical quotations, and well
you know it. But my mother always used to say:
'Sufficient unto the day is the evil thereof.'
Which is just another way of saying you can
start afresh in the morning.
Nurse Crane *Series 7, Episode 4*

Hope. It's the best thing of all.
Dr Turner *Series 5, Episode 5*

Not so long ago, I thought I'd never be
happy again. And yet here I am. The human
heart really is most resilient.
Trixie *Series 7, Episode 2*

The longest paths lead into sunlight,
when they are paved with love.
Narration by Jennifer *Series 7, Episode 2*

Dr Turner I don't know what's worse. Hope, like those little boys had. Or no hope at all.
Shelagh There's never no hope at all, Patrick. It's 1962! *Series 6, Christmas Special*

Then I'm just going to say one thing, and you can dismiss it as platitude if you prefer. But I generally find that if you can summon the courage to sit through the bleakest day, then in the end the weather will change. You just have to hope that when the sun comes out you aren't wearing wellington boots and a sou'wester, because there's nothing worse than being wrongly dressed for an occasion.
Trixie *Series 6, Episode 6*

My mother – when there was a storm – she used to be sure to open the front door and the back door. So the thunder and lightning would go straight through. Don't let your misfortunes find a home, she'd tell me.
Maurice Glennon *Series 3, Episode 6*

This is
the dark before
the dawn, but there
is always a dawn.
Sister Winifred
Series 6, Episode 2

MEMORIES

I am not deemed capable of coherent recollection.
But some things are etched upon my membrane;
they are preserved like watermarks on vellum.
Sister Monica Joan *Series 1, Episode 1*

Dr Turner A lot of memories.
Timothy Yes.
Dr Turner They don't belong to the house.
They're ours. They come with us. *Series 6, Episode 6*

We are not defined by the things that make
us separate and distinct, but by the moments that
we share, and the memories we make. And we
are shaped by the hands we hold in ours,
and cherish, and gently let go.
Narration by Jennifer *Series 4, Episode 6*

The fears we have in the present often lie
in the experiences of the past.
Sister Winifred *Series 7, Episode 2*

SOLITUDE

Sometimes solitude is the best society.
Sister Monica Joan

Series 7, Episode 6

There's only so much peace and quiet
a soul can take – in the end, it's like giving
a plant too much water.
Sister Evangelina *Series 5, Episode 7*

PART FOUR

THE JOY OF LIFE

BEAUTY

You'll have to excuse me, I'm going to make
myself a face mask out of salad cream. I believe
one can find the most amazing aids to beauty
in the kitchen cupboards.
Trixie *Series 5, Episode 4*

From the extreme height of your heels,
I deduce that you are not a nun.
Sister Monica Joan *Series 1, Episode 1*

Even a modest risk to life and limb is better
than blonde hair poking through one's hosiery.
Trixie *Series 9, Episode 1*

The transformative powers of silk. Day to night in
an instant. You can thank me later with a Babycham.
Trixie *Series 3, Episode 2*

Much is ruined in pursuit of self-improvement.
Narration by Jennifer *Series 9, Episode 2*

What do we see, when we look in the mirror?
Our truest selves, or a faint approximation of
someone we'd rather be? The mirror sees it all.
Our fears, our little triumphs. And keeps our
secrets, holds our disappointments in.
Narration by Jennifer *Series 4, Episode 8*

Chummy The day has dawned.
Arrange a toll of bells.
PC Noakes What's happening?
Chummy I can't get my girdle on.
PC Noakes D'you want me to pull on the straps?
Chummy Peter, Charles Atlas could pull on the
straps and they'd never meet across this tum!
Series 2, Episode 8

Where immortality is concerned,
the coiffure is an irrelevance.
Sister Monica Joan *Series 7, Episode 4*

Please don't dismiss vanity,
it's one of my most salient features.
Trixie *Series 9, Episode 5*

The trouble with poodle skirts is they can't be worn with a straight face any more. You need a dash of irony, or you'll simply look naive.
Trixie *Series 4, Episode 6*

Jenny At least I don't pretend to be a natural blonde.
Trixie No pretence – I can assure you. My mother said I was born with a halo.

Series 3, Episode 2

I think it's insanity trying to change our hairdos in the middle of the week. I set my hair on the weekend, and then I just add more lacquer on a daily basis. The H-bomb couldn't budge it by the weekend.
Valerie

Series 8, Episode 4

Miss Higgins Do you suppose Her Majesty
has a permanent wave, or a shampoo and set?
Her coiffure always looks so very crisp.
Shelagh Oh, I think a permanent wave, don't you?
The Queen always strikes me as a very efficient
sort of person. Not one to waste time with a
hairdresser every day!

Series 8, Episode 1

Mater would thoroughly approve of this. She
always wanted me to slenderise, then when she was
dying, she pushed a plate of scones towards me and
said, 'Camilla. Look after your face. The other end's
for sitting on, nobody will ever see it.'

Chummy *Series 4, Episode 8*

We're going to a French place. And if it's French,
they'll serve snails, and snails always involve bent
pins, garlic butter and finger bowls. Which, all in all,
means quite a lot of attention on one's manicure.

Trixie *Series 6, Episode 5*

I had quite serious intentions about this hairdo! I didn't spend five shillings on setting lotion and two hours in rollers only to spend the evening knitting with the nuns.
Trixie
Series 6, Episode 7

PC Noakes What do they actually do up there for so long?
Alec Mysterious, fragrant things that can't be rushed. *Series 3, Episode 3*

Magda, the au pair At school they told us nail polish was the worst kind of Western decadence.
Trixie They're quite wrong. It's the very best kind. *Series 7, Episode 3*

An elegant woman wears her clothes, they don't wear her.
Trixie *Series 5, Episode 1*

SUMMER

Who can forget the return to work and school
after the summer? Immaculate shoes, the
pristine pencil case, the promise that this year
homework would be done on time,
in absolutely perfect writing.
Narration by Jennifer *Series 7, Episode 6*

I much prefer the cold. I find it keeps the mind sharper.
Miss Higgins *Series 8, Episode 4*

The month of May comes differently in cities.
Not for us white blossom on the hedgerows,
and bluebells in the woods. Instead, the sun's
rays burnish bricks, and mellow pavements.
Seeds burst into flower in the cracks between
the stones, and speedwell and bindweed bloom
among the rubble.
Narration by Jennifer *Series 9, Episode 3*

TRAVEL

What are horizons for, if not to be expanded?
Nurse Crane *Series 8, Episode 4*

I always read my maps upside down.
It's an absolutely infallible way of working
out left and right.
Trixie *Series 9, Christmas Special*

If you're going to slow to a dead stop every time
a specimen of the local wildlife hoves into view,
we won't attain our objective this side of Christmas!
Nurse Crane *Series 9, Christmas Special*

Sister Winifred I'm awfully sorry. But has
anybody got anything for sunburn? I think my
forehead's starting to blister.
Nurse Crane Oh, surely it wasn't that hot?
Sister Winifred No. But underneath all of this,
I'm a redhead.
Nurse Crane Your eyebrows had given rise
to speculation.
Series 6, Christmas Special

Some travel geographically, trading home for home, and one language for another. But we all move from youth to maturity, childhood to parenthood, as if we were traversing continents. The world shifts, and the climate alters. Safe passage cannot be bought, and we have no holy passport to protect us. And so we venture forward, fragile maps in hand. Flying our banners of courage, and of hope.
Narration by Jennifer *Series 6, Episode 3*

FOOD AND TREATS

Sister Julienne Sister Monica Joan,
you haven't had the swiss roll.
Sister Monica Joan I cannot excite myself
about a fatless sponge. It is principally air,
and I feel untethered by it.

Series 2, Episode 1

Patsy Oh, Lord! Is that lemon meringue pie?
Chummy Sorry, old thing. It's spoken for.
It's been promised as a raffle prize.
Trixie Can we turn our minds to the Jubilee buffet?
We're going to have vol-au-vents, and cheese
and pineapple sticks.
Cynthia Are you sure, Trixie? Sister Evangelina's
got quite a conservative palate.
Trixie And butterfly cakes, and a sherry trifle.
Oh, and I've found a recipe for the most marvellous
centrepiece. Do look. It's called a banana coronet.
Patsy It looks a bit like Stonehenge.
Only made of penises.

Series 3, Episode 5

You're like a moth to a flame with meringue, you needn't think we've forgotten the Queen of Puddings!
Sister Evangelina
Series 3, Episode 5

Don't go putting any Bourbons out.
They create expectations that we'll struggle to fulfill.
Sister Evangelina *Series 2, Christmas Special*

Tea, and a plate of bread and butter.
There's absolutely nothing like it when one's
been up since the small hours.
Sister Hilda *Series 8, Episode 8*

Delia Violet's jam. First of the year.
Barbara Yes, please.
Nurse Crane I believe there's similar excitement
in France with the arrival of the Beaujolais.
Series 6, Episode 3

There's something about hovering on the brink
of a nuclear war that rather blunts the appetite.
Delia *Series 6, Episode 6*

I shall not partake of crumpets.
They are too multicellular, and too spongiform.
And, in this case, they are too cold.
Sister Monica Joan *Series 6, Episode 8*

Liqueur chocolates, how decadent!
And a urine sample! You are kind.
Trixie *Series 3, Christmas Special*

There are only three rules when planning an intimate dinner party. The food should be cooked to perfection, and presented with style. And the guests should be agreeable.
Trixie *Series 7, Episode 2*

Tea. The drink that enlivens and reanimates.
Sister Monica Joan *Series 9, Episode 5*

I reckon we've earned more than toast. There's half a chocolate button cake in a tin in the bottom cupboard, have a look at the back behind the All-Bran.
Sister Evangelina *Series 5, Episode 8*

Cynthia Does anyone else's sherry taste of toothpaste?
Trixie We're drinking out of tooth mugs. Close your eyes and pretend it's crème de menthe.
Series 1, Episode 6

EXERCISE

Daily practice is the key for exercise.
Nurse Crane *Series 8, Episode 4*

It's most unwise to come to a Keep Fit class
without having had anything to eat.
Trixie *Series 8, Episode 4*

Trixie The reason this exercise is called The Flamingo
is because whilst one leg bears the entire weight of
the body, the other is fully extended behind.
Violet It's not because we're all turning pink, then?
Series 6, Episode 4

Oh gosh, it seems I'm going to a dance.
Voluntarily. 'Look at me now, Ma.'
Chummy *Series 1, Episode 4*

The waltz is all about protection. It's a dance
that says: 'I have you in my arms, my dear,
all is well with the world.'
Fred *Series 3, Episode 7*

I started coming to Keep Fit at an absolutely ghastly time in my life. It meant that for an hour or two each week, I didn't have to think about all the horrible and wretched things that made me so frightfully unhappy. But after a while, Keep Fit didn't just distract me, it started to make me stronger. And what's more, I've lost two inches from around my waist, and gone up a whole cup size in the bra department. This really is the very best thing I've ever done.

Trixie

Series 5, Episode 1

CHRISTMAS

Dr Turner Most people spend their Christmas Day afternoon watching Billy Smart's Circus and eating Quality Street! How have we ended up discussing a mission to South Africa?
Shelagh Because God moves in a mysterious manner. Even on major public holidays.
Series 6, Christmas Special

There are always angels, everywhere. Perhaps we only think to look for them at Christmas, when their wings can be seen, when their halos glow with light. But they are always there. There in the quiet corners, there in the shadows, there in their ordinary clothes, and they are beautiful. Make room for the angels. And their gifts will fill your heart in ways you never can imagine.
Narration by Jennifer *Series 8, Christmas Special*

Sometimes Christmas is not a still point. Snow swirls, and melts away, and the day doesn't offer up the peace that we imagined. But in the darkness, seeds awake, and green shoots unfurl towards the light.
Narration by Jennifer *Series 3, Christmas Special*

But the very purpose of Christmas is to revisit where one's roots lie! Was Christ himself not born in Bethlehem because his father and mother were called to their birthplace for the census? All should head homeward, if their natal home still stands.
Sister Monica Joan *Series 5, Christmas Special*

Year by year by year, we share the season and move on. There will always be another Christmas, and all will be well. All will be well.
Narration by Jennifer *Series 7, Christmas Special*

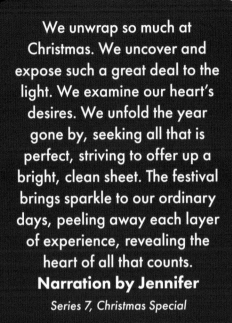

We unwrap so much at Christmas. We uncover and expose such a great deal to the light. We examine our heart's desires. We unfold the year gone by, seeking all that is perfect, striving to offer up a bright, clean sheet. The festival brings sparkle to our ordinary days, peeling away each layer of experience, revealing the heart of all that counts.

Narration by Jennifer

Series 7, Christmas Special

Call me a stickler for the Scriptures, but I don't recall any reindeer in Bethlehem.

Sister Hilda

Series 9, Christmas Special

When autumn starts to dampen into winter, should we say, 'The nights are getting dark'? Should we thrust our hands into our pockets and anticipate the chill? Or should we say, 'Light the fire. Draw close. It will not be as cold as you imagine.'
Narration by Jennifer *Series 9, Episode 8*

Christmas is the celebration of a baby's birth. It is the story of a mother's love, her fear, her faith and her determination. It tells of promises fulfilled, a cradle rocked, a journey both concluded and begun. It is the story of all that is cherished.
Narration by Jennifer *Series 5, Christmas Special*

Some Christmases will always be more memorable than others. More joyful, more serene, replete with blessings, and with love. 'That,' we will say, 'was the best Christmas ever.' We unbox our traditions, year by year. Each celebration must compete with all of those that went before.

Narration by Jennifer *Series 9, Christmas Special*

We set high standards, write long lists. We cannot be ill. We cannot afford to falter. Christmas becomes a challenge we must rise to. It is our duty to burnish it and to make it shine. We must do well. We must be well. We must do the best we can.

Narration by Jennifer *Series 9, Christmas Special*

The most precious gifts cost nothing whatsoever.
Narration by Jennifer *Series 6, Christmas Special*

WISDOM OF AGE

Like the temples of Thebes I crumble,
my needs reviewed with every passing year.
The time of being useful, the time of being important,
these too have passed.
Sister Monica Joan *Series 2, Episode 2*

It sometimes seems to me the older I get,
the more I have to learn.
Sister Julienne *Series 5, Christmas Special*

Newborns are always beautiful. They cannot
fail to make the heart sing, for even the plainest
faces are alive with promise. But I have always
seen beauty in old age too. Light shines through
the bone, exquisite even as it flickers. Even as it
flutters, and dims, towards the end.
Narration by Jennifer *Series 1, Episode 6*

> The young cannot see what lies ahead, and perhaps that is their blessing, and their sorrow.
> **Narration by Jennifer** *Series 3, Episode 8*

Sister Bernadette We love Sister Monica Joan, Doctor, and we do the best we can for her. But it wouldn't be right to lock her in her room! Besides, the truth is, we don't know whether she has dementia or whether she's just wilfully eccentric!

Dr Turner I understand. There are more medical treatises written about senile decay than you can shake a stick at, but I keep to one invariable diagnostic rule: if they're brought back by a policeman, in their nightie, then they've got it.

Series 1, Episode 6

I hope, that when our own use is concluded, we are not all faced with cremation in a dustbin.
Sister Monica Joan *Series 8, Episode 1*

I think you'll find that old instruments – if they are of good quality – retain their value and purpose. Neither this reliable globe nor I, though both 'old instruments', are by any means redundant.
Sister Monica Joan *Series 3, Episode 6*

I daren't even look in the mirror with my glasses on. My whole face is sort of sliding downwards, like a rather exhausted blancmange.
Chummy *Series 4, Episode 8*

God once said to Saint Peter, 'When you are young, you go where you wish. When you are old, others will take you where you do not wish to go.'
Sister Julienne *Series 1, Episode 3*

I shall be eternally glad when I am transmogrified; the burden of the flesh is so heavy it is no marvel that the soul feels trapped.
Sister Monica Joan *Series 4, Episode 8*

YOUTH

When we are young, there is always more to be embraced. More energy. More Joy. More opportunity to flourish. We live life in forward motion, surging ahead. Eyes aimed at the horizon. And even hard labour, and sacrifice, feel worthwhile when offered up as down payment on the future.
Narration by Jennifer *Series 8, Episode 4*

To the young it seems no door is closed, and as though all hearts are open. Everything is possible. And love comes so easily.
Narration by Jennifer *Series 3, Episode 4*

PART FIVE

SIGNS OF THE TIMES

WOMEN'S WORK

Oh we must always live as we please – so long as no one gets hurt in the process. Recklessness is quite another matter. But these are wonderful days, girls. Go out there and take hold of them! You're not given opportunities. You grab them. With both hands.
Nurse Crane *Series 5, Episode 2*

Gentle persuasion is often more effective than a heavy hand.
Sister Monica Joan *Series 8, Episode 5*

I feel sorry for Princess Margaret. Imagine having to look enthralled by someone boiling urine.
Trixie *Series 3, Episode 1*

You cannot launder woollens using electrical apparatus! The fibres will become disordered, and the very essence of the garment lost.
Sister Monica Joan *Series 4, Episode 2*

Until you girls with all your training, and all your learning, sort something out with the men who make the law, there'll be names being whispered, and money changing hands in every back street in England. Because when lives go wrong, we can put them right.

Elsie *Series 8, Episode 8*

I sometimes wonder what the last two wars were for in that respect. Every time the world goes up in flames, they draft women in to pick up the slack and then once it's over, it's, 'Back in your box and don't say boo.'

Nurse Crane *Series 4, Episode 4*

The trouble is, Peter, I'm a midwife. And babies aren't exactly a part-time business.

Chummy *Series 3, Episode 5*

Oh, we have a head! And that, Rhoda Mullucks, is why women ought to run this country!

Patsy *Series 5, Episode 1*

Jeannie was unhappy. Jeannie was frightened. Jeannie did not want to have a baby. And I can tell you that we see this all the time! Young, young girls. Exhausted, older women. Mothers who don't know where their next penny, or their next beating's coming from, and others who want to take control of their bodies, and their lives. And all we can do is pat them on the hand, and say, 'You'll manage, everybody does.' But not everybody does! Not everybody believes us.

Trixie *Series 8, Episode 4*

A woman is defined by her potential, and not her circumstances.

Trixie

Series 8, Christmas Special

Sister Monica Joan The punishment
is not ours to administer.
Sister Frances But can't the anger be ours to feel?
Series 8, Episode 8

It's peculiar, isn't it? We can be so very organised
in our work yet so chaotic in our lives. I found a pair
of Freddie's booties in the larder this morning.
It's only a matter of time before I start using
Peter's police helmet as a coal scuttle.
Chummy *Series 3, Episode 2*

Wool-crafts are the refuge of a dull mind.
Sister Monica Joan *Series 7, Episode 2*

Women write their history in the words that pass between them. Too often, they leave no trace beyond the children born, the clothing stitched, the service given, the choices made – if there was choice at all. But in 1961, we were choosing routes, and taking byways never walked before. We did not hesitate, or stumble, because all roads were unexplored, and everything was possible.

Narration by Jennifer *Series 5, Episode 8*

Fred And finally, what would you do to bring about world peace?
Valerie I'd put a Poplar woman in charge. Anyone who's seen my auntie at closing time on a Saturday knows – we don't put up with any messing.

Series 7, Episode 3

ON MEN

My mother always said: 'Find a plain man,
he'll be eternally grateful and never stray.'
Nurse Crane *Series 4, Episode 3*

My Sisters and I will not want to come in
here ever again and find the seat of a
certain item standing upright!
Sister Evangelina *Series 2, Episode 8*

Mrs Buckle,
I haven't seen my
mother for a year or two, but
she would always talk about a
woman's intuition. And what I say is
this – where men are concerned,
sometimes a woman's intuition doesn't
get her anywhere. You need to let
the men talk to the men. Let them
sort it out themselves.
Cyril *Series 8, Episode 8*

Patsy With the greatest respect,
Tom is not my type. At all.
Trixie What do you mean by that?
Patsy Well, apart from the fact that he's clearly
besotted with you, there are certain things he lacks
and certain things he has too much of. For me.
Series 3, Episode 7

The Bible had a plague of locusts, we have a
plague of pensioners! Scarcely a crumb left in
their wake, and I'm sorry to say that I've just
had my bottom pinched.
Trixie *Series 5, Episode 6*

It's easy to overburden a man. They think they
must give the impression of being more substantial
than they actually are.
Nurse Crane *Series 7, Episode 2*

You are no better than Plato, who believed
a woman's womb would roam her body,
provoking psychological disease. I have put
Plato here, next to Mr Freud, so they can be
companions in their ignorance.
Sister Monica Joan *Series 3, Episode 1*

One always hopes there might be some
sort of a chap along the way.
Chummy *Series 1, Episode 2*

All I would say is, men in the delivery room are
a lot like gas and air. When it comes to the crunch,
you might change your opinion.
Nurse Crane *Series 9, Episode 8*

Trixie Fred has a wide range of sidelines,
some of which are actually legal.
Fred You can keep your aspersions to
yourself, young madam.
Trixie I'm not complaining. We thoroughly
enjoyed your alcoholic ginger beer.
Cynthia It was just a shame you sold some
to those children. *Series 1, Episode 1*

She wouldn't kill him. No mother ever did.
She would only curse his name, and say there'd
never be a next time. And she would mean it.
And there always was.
Narration by Jennifer *Series 1, Episode 2*

We strove to serve women, living alongside and amongst them. Men were creatures that you married, or marvelled at, yearned for, or found somehow perplexing. Mainly, they made work for us, and we knew no rest.
Narration by Jennifer *Series 2, Episode 1*

Doing what he wants isn't the same as doing what's best.
Cynthia *Series 2, Episode 7*

Trixie All the same, I'm baffled that *anyone* thinks that girls aren't the equal of boys.
Patsy I don't think they're the equal of boys. I think they're better.
Series 4, Episode 4

Well, I'm hardly an expert when it comes to men, but I'm fairly sure that chocolate usually takes the edge off when things go wrong.
Cynthia *Series 3, Episode 3*

If a man can help his wife with childcare,
then she might also get some time to relax
when the baby comes.
Valerie *Series 7, Episode 2*

Not every husband has the stomach for childbirth.
A man's job isn't to guide his child through the
birth canal, but through life itself!
Nurse Crane *Series 7, Episode 2*

Maudie Valentine Didn't you ever want a fella?
Sister Monica Joan Jason held a fleeting appeal.
But Odysseus was my one true love.
Maudie Valentine Local boy, was he?
Sister Monica Joan He felt so to me.
Maudie Valentine But you chose the Church.
Sister Monica Joan I chose a life of service.
And study. And the freedom to pursue both.
For me, marriage would have been a jail.
Series 7, Episode 6

Nurse Crane I've met countless lads like
Ronald before. He needs some friendly advice.
Not to interfere. Not to panic. He needs to learn that,
rather like your relationship with your father, some
things just are. And we can do nothing about it.
Sister Hilda We have a saying about that.
'Go with God.'
Nurse Crane Doris Day has another.
'Que sera, sera.'
Series 9, Episode 5

Men. I should've known better than to trust one.
You're all talk. Never owning up. Blaming everyone
else. It doesn't matter whether you've got a big
fancy job like you or whether you're like Vic,
without a pot to piss in. You're all the same
underneath. The same scared little boys.
Yvonne Smith *Series 9, Episode 7*

Shutting maternity homes across the country,
whatever next? Only a man could think it's
a good idea.
Nurse Crane *Series 6, Episode 3*

I blame the films. Makes girls go mad for romance and roses and Rossano bloody Brazzi!
Zelda *Series 6, Episode 1*

Becoming a father is wonderful, but it's also the biggest responsibility you will ever have to shoulder.
Dr Turner *Series 8, Episode 7*

Trixie, there are some women who make a very decent fist of being spinsters. I like to think I'm one of them, and – if we sidestep the small detail of her marriage to Jesus – so was Sister Evangelina. But you aren't, and there's no use pretending otherwise.
Nurse Crane
Series 5, Episode 8

CHANGING TIMES

If it's about this contraceptive pill, all I've got to say is, it's typical of Doctor Turner. One sniff of a novelty medication, he's off like a moggie with catmint.
Sister Evangelina *Series 5, Episode 7*

Oh, I don't know about these American pop groups. There's such a lot of slang in their songs, and their diction leaves a lot to be desired!
Shelagh *Series 7, Episode 1*

There is always change, everywhere.
And the circle of love is not broken, it expands.
Narration by Jennifer *Series 6, Episode 8*

We can never foretell when our fortunes will turn, or when the story will change.
Narration by Jennifer *Series 8, Episode 7*

Dr Turner The Sisters of Nonnatus are an integral part of this community. Always have been.
Sister Julienne Being part of the furniture does not equate to our security, Doctor Turner.
Series 9, Episode 4

Best advice I ever received? When in the path of an unstoppable force, it's always best to surrender.
Nurse Crane *Series 4, Episode 3*

Time isn't always a healer. But it can open doors.
Dr Turner *Series 7, Episode 5*

I've never been one to eschew a fresh experience.
And I shall enjoy the chance to utilise the parking
meter system. One must remain in step with the times.
Nurse Crane *Series 8, Episode 4*

I am determined for us to keep our presence here. But
the times are changing, Doctor Turner. If we do not
change with them, I fear we may become obsolete.
Sister Julienne *Series 9, Episode 4*

I've lived through two world wars and the Blitz —
but I think Julie Andrews might just polish me off.
Sister Evangelina *Series 3, Episode 3*

Dr Turner Sister, there isn't an ashtray in my cubicle.
Jenny I'll fetch one right away, Doctor.
Series 3, Episode 4

Change is not loss. We must run with it.
Dance with it. Give it all we have.
Narration by Jennifer *Series 9, Episode 5*

Our world was moving from the time of limits and austerity into one which promised endless reinvention. We could change the homes we lived in, and the clothes we bought. We could fly across the world, investigate new planets, begin to crack our own genetic code. But no matter what science sought, our challenge remained the same. To accept what it meant to be human. To embrace our strengths, our weaknesses, our dreams.
Narration by Jennifer *Series 6, Episode 2*

Barbara Toy Box Corner was left unsupervised for one minute, and Susan pushed a piece of Lego up her nose. I can't get it out!
Sister Evangelina Lego? Used to be dried peas and Meccano screws. Still, least we're moving with the times. *Series 4, Episode 6*

We cannot stand still, because the world keeps turning. Every year must give way to the next, and its stories must be folded. Tucked away like children's clothes — outgrown, cherished, and never quite forgotten.

Narration by Jennifer *Series 6, Episode 8*

A woman of substance can make a home anywhere. And you, Miss Millgrove, are a woman of substance.
Lucille
Series 8, Episode 2

Marlene, Fred's daughter Every time I come home, there's another gap where something used to be.

Fred Ain't that the truth. Sometimes I think it's only the river that stays the same. *Series 4, Episode 8*

Sister Monica Joan There is much of value in the old ways.

Nurse Crane Exactly!

Sister Monica Joan But one must not become like Lot's wife – frozen in the act of looking backwards.

Series 7, Episode 2

The past is never lost to us. We carry it with us, everywhere we go. It is in every cell of our body and our soul. It is where we have been. It is where we learn to love. It is where we made our mistakes. The gift is knowing that the present will soon pass, and that the way we embrace it has the power to change everything.

Narration by Jennifer *Series 9, Episode 1*

Familiarity need not breed contempt. A new adventure, or a special dress, can render the mundane bright and the accustomed novel. Sometimes, we simply see each other through fresh eyes. And there is joy in it.
Narration by Jennifer *Series 8, Episode 7*

Trixie On my next day off I'm going to buy myself a pair of pantyhose.
Nurse Crane 'Pantyhose'? What on earth are 'pantyhose'?
Barbara They're a new kind of suspender-less stocking! They've had them in America for years.
Nurse Crane You make that sound like a recommendation.
Trixie But think, Phyllis! No metal clips, no buttons, no belts. Nothing digging in. Just silky, whisper-light nylon clinging like a second skin from waist to toe.
Nurse Crane Sounds like a breeding ground for yeast. *Series 5, Episode 8*

Mrs Leonard The Yanks reckon they've got a pill stops you getting in the family way.
Trixie That's Hollywood for you – full of happy endings.
Mrs Leonard Give us a pill that makes fellas do the washing up.

Series 1, Episode 5

Nothing stays the same. We don't stay the same ourselves. And all the time, the world keeps on spinning faster.
Sister Evangelina

Series 5, Episode 7

We're all meant to be travelling forwards. Everything's supposed to be improving, all the time.
Shelagh *Series 9, Episode 1*

THE EAST END

Pearl Winston I bet you think we're all
slatterns round here, don't you?
Jenny As a matter of fact, I think you're all heroines.
Series 1, Episode 1

Poverty isn't bad housing, dirty clothing, families of
ten. It's never having been loved, or even respected.
Not knowing the difference between love and abuse,
a kiss that wasn't down payment on a blow.
Father Joe *Series 1, Episode 2*

The River Thames pulsed through the heart of
the East End like its blood. Sustaining its people,
and taking with it much they had thrown away
or lost. For some it marked the beginning of a
journey. For others it became a channel of return,
bringing back the missing and the loved, the
forgotten and the longed for. It was often an
escape route and sometimes the road home.
Narration by Jennifer *Series 2, Episode 7*

I must have been mad. I could have been an air hostess. I could have been a model. I could have moved to Paris, or been a concert pianist. I could have seen the world, been brave, followed my heart. But I didn't. I side-stepped love, and set off for the East End of London. Because I thought it would be easier. Madness was the only explanation.

Narration by Jennifer *Series 1, Episode 1*

Cynthia The first time I saw an East End bathroom, I actually shook.
Trixie Bathroom? You were lucky! *Series 1, Episode 1*

I saw a thousand dawns when I was working in the East End. A thousand fresh beginnings, every day a world made new. There were challenges, and changes, but always the sense of life forging forward, pulsing like the River Thames itself.

Narration by Jennifer *Series 3, Episode 1*

At least we'll be in the same boat as everyone else round here. Everyone's up to their eyes in rubble, and nobody knows what the future holds. We're just going to have to carry on.
Valerie *Series 9, Episode 6*

Sister Julienne When I was new to district practice, I often found it hard to conquer my revulsion.
Jenny I'm sorry. I didn't know people lived like this.
Sister Julienne But they do. And it's why we're here.
Series 1, Episode 1

In the East End, I found grace, and faith, and hope hidden in the darkest corners. I found tenderness in squalor, and laughter amid filth. I found a purpose, and a path, and I worked with a passion, for the best reason of all. I did it for love.
Narration by Jennifer *Series 1, Episode 6*

MANNERS

When I was in training, we were always taught
to say, 'Good morning', 'Good afternoon' or 'Good
evening'. 'Hello' would not have been permitted.
Unless we were talking to Americans, perhaps.
Nurse Crane *Series 4, Episode 2*

I am always wary of the phrase 'with respect',
Nurse Anderson. I generally find it is a forerunner
to candour, or possibly impertinence.
Sister Julienne *Series 7, Episode 2*

I'm afraid I don't care if you don't like potted
beef, Dean. Once you've bitten into it,
you can't put it back.
Nurse Crane *Series 7, Episode 5*

She was a grafter, and grafters don't waste
time on pleasantries.
Fred *Series 5, Episode 8*

No one is ever late in God's eyes.
Alecia Palmer *Series 7, Episode 7*

Sometimes the act of letter writing is as
important as the receipt of the letter.
Sister Julienne *Series 3, Episode 2*

Sorry. I have an uncanny knack for misplaced jollity.
Feel free to shy a plimsoll at me.
Chummy *Series 4, Episode 8*

ADVICE FOR LIFE

Gathered together, we find our light.
And each spark shifts and multiplies, scattering
its radiance on our ordinary lives. Like everything
precious, more valuable when shared. Like every
common miracle, made of the stuff of stars.
Let the light shine. Watch for it falling on each
other's faces. Count the beams, catch them, let
them be reflected back. See the hope, see the
promise. Never hide your fears in silence.
Listen to those you cherish, hold them in your
arms. Let them hear your heart. Tell your truth.
Tell your story. Tell your love.
Narration by Jennifer *Series 8, Episode 8*